This book
BELONGS
to

LOVE
IS LIKE A
RAINBOW
JUST ADD
WATER

THUNDER BAY
P·R·E·S·S
San Diego, California

Thunder Bay P·R·E·S·S

Thunder Bay Press
An imprint of Printers Row Publishing Group
10350 Barnes Canyon Road, Suite 100
San Diego, CA 92121
www.thunderbaybooks.com

Printers Row Publishing Group is a division of
Readerlink Distribution Services, LLC. Thunder
Bay Press is a registered trademark of Readerlink
Distribution Services, LLC.

All notations of errors or omissions should be
addressed to Thunder Bay Press, Editorial
Department, at the above address. All other
correspondence (author inquiries, permissions)
concerning the content of this book should be
addressed to Quarto Publishing plc.

Conceived, edited, and designed by
Quarto Publishing plc,
6 Blundell Street, London, N7 9BH, UK.

QUAR.325425

Thunder Bay Press
Publisher: Peter Norton
Associate Publisher: Ana Parker
Publishing/Editorial Team: Kathryn C. Dalby,
April Farr, Kelly Larsen
Editorial Team: JoAnn Padgett, Melinda Allman,
Dan Mansfield

Quarto Publishing
Senior Art Editor: Emma Clayton
Art Director: Gemma Wilson
Illustrator: Kuo Kang Chen
Editorial Assistant: Charlene Fernandes
Publisher: Samantha Warrington

ISBN: 978-1-64517-145-4

Manufactured in Malaysia

23 22 21 20 19   1 2 3 4 5

CREDITS

Vasilisa Kryuchkova/Shutterstock.com;
sailorlun/Shutterstock.com; M_Morozova/
Shutterstock.com; Iveta Angelova/
Shutterstock.com; Big Boy/Shutterstock.com;
Bimbim/Shutterstock.com; Giuseppe_R/
Shutterstock.com; S.Bunya/Shutterstock.com;
nani888/Shutterstock.com; Eva Kali/
Shutterstock.com; vendor/Shutterstock.com;
OlichO/Shutterstock.com; ImHope/
Shutterstock.com; Mjosedesign/Shutterstock.
com; YAZZIK/Shutterstock.com; Alka5051/
Shutterstock.com; Lightkite/Shutterstock.com;
Helen Lane/Shutterstock.com; Bronitskaya/
Shutterstock.com; sliplee/Shutterstock.com;
Toporovska Nataliia/Shutterstock.com;
HitToon/Shutterstock.com; Elina Li/
Shutterstock.com; Imagepluss/Shutterstock.
com; tanvetka/Shutterstock.com; Doodle
flower/Shutterstock.com; Tina Bits/
Shutterstock.com; Vesnin_Sergey/
Shutterstock.com; Norrapat Thepnarin/
Shutterstock.com; panki/Shutterstock.com;
mis-Tery/Shutterstock.com; MG Drachal/
Shutterstock.com; Yeresko Natali /
Shutterstock.com; Slanapotam/Shutterstock.
com; Verock/Shutterstock.com; Cute art/
Shutterstock.com; chyworks/Shutterstock.
com; NadiiaZ/Shutterstock.com; vector_ann/
Shutterstock.com; maritel/Shutterstock.com;
Khaneeros/Shutterstock.com; Helen_st/
Shutterstock.com; Keiti/Shutterstock.com;
Suwi19 /Shutterstock.com; natsa/Shutterstock.
com; Epine/Shutterstock.com; Bokasana/
Shutterstock.com; H Art/Shutterstock.com;
ksugas/Shutterstock.com; Oksana Lysak/
Shutterstock.com;
Anchalee Ar/Shutterstock.com

KEY

· · · · · · · · ·

WET ME WITH WATER AND THE BRUSH
SUPPLIED, AND WATCH THE COLORS EMERGE

COLOR ME WITH PENCILS,
PENS, OR MARKERS

About This Book

· · · · · · · · · · · · · · ·

This book contains life-affirming statements illustrated with fabulous art that requires no more than the application of a wet paintbrush to spring to life! Start by selecting an affirmation that best matches how you want to feel (experts say that repeating positive mantras can reprogram your subconscious mind and encourage feelings of well-being and positivity). Look in the page margin to see if the subject is a "magic painting" or one that requires dry media to color it in. Then follow the instructions below.

🜄 MAGIC PAINTING

1 Slip the back cover flap beneath your chosen painting to prevent water from seeping through.

2 Dip the brush tip in clean water and gently apply the brush to the black linework. Follow the lines. Avoid overwetting the artwork. Relax! Take your time. Watch as different colors emerge and mix together on the page. Carefully tear out your painting along the perforated edge.

3 Leave the painting to dry flat. Then put it on display!

TRADITIONAL COLORING-IN

1 Slip the back cover flap beneath your chosen picture to prevent the images beneath from being dented, if you press down heavily with your color pencils.

2 Choose between pencils, pens, or markers. When working with color pencils, build up rich and varied color effects by mixing colored pencils on the paper surface. Vary the pressure of the pencil point to affect the depth of color.

3 Once your artwork is complete, carefully tear out the page along the perforated edge. Then put it on display!

LOVE
is an
ART

There are MANY WAYS
to spread more LOVE

SOMEWHERE, someone is THINKING of me and SMILING

As I wake each morning, I celebrate the love in my life

Embracing love ...

... is my biggest adventure

Love
EMBELLISHES LIFE with
NEVER-ENDING Beauty

LOVE IS ART that comes from ★THE **HEART**

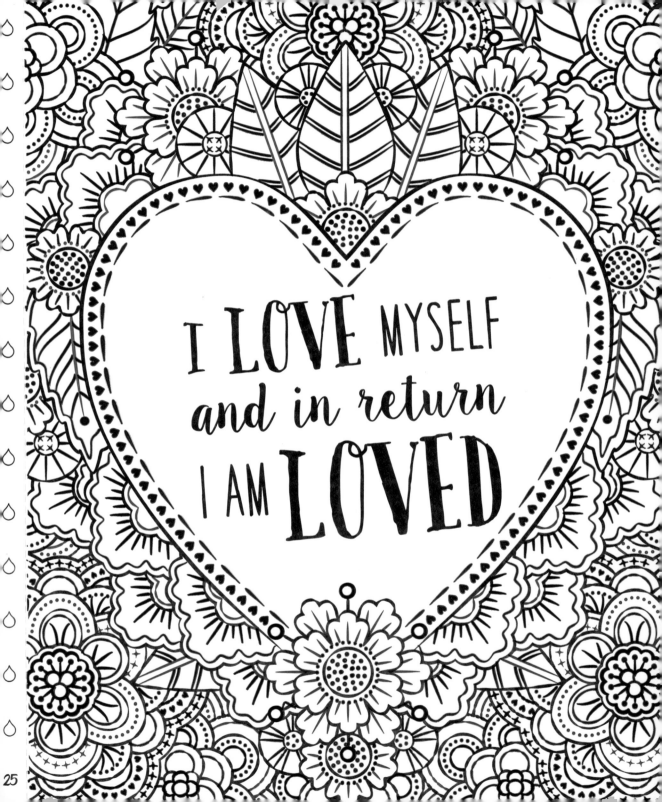

I am enough

I let **love** LIGHT the way

AND GUIDE me on my *journey*

I am **WORTHY** OF
a peaceful and calm
LIFE

True love
unfolds when nothing
is looked for in
return

Real LOVE is worth the WAIT

Love makes **two hearts** become **one**

BE A
RAINBOW
to someone else's
CLOUD

All you need is *love*

and a whole *heap* of *ice cream!*

As I close my eyes each night,

I give thanks for the joys for the joys love brings each day

When I **love** someone, their HAPPINESS is my *happiness*

Everywhere I go I find love

THERE IS NO LIMIT to what I can achieve

3

I see **myself** filled

with *love* and *happiness*

A sea of love washes over me
and fills me with joy

I ALLOW *love* to come to me

I WILL LET *love* find me

Home is where the heart is

WHEN IT RAINS, always look for RAINBOWS

I choose to share
my love generously

I follow my *heart*

as I follow my *dreams*

When we are ★ MILES apart, ★

I KNOW we are close in heart

I trust that the *universe* will bring me supporting, *loving relationships*

I deserve a **stable** *and* **HAPPY** relationship

Be bright and positive

and spread seeds of love

I am BLESSED that my WORLD ...

... iS FILLED With LOVE